THE ÆSOP FOR CHILDREN

THE COCK AND THE FOX

The ÆSOP for CHILDREN

WITH PICTURES BY MILO WINTER

RAND McNALLY & CO.
CHICAGO

A LIST OF THE FABLES

THE WOLF AND THE KID

THE ÆSOP FOR CHILDREN

THE WOLF AND THE KID

There was once a little Kid whose growing horns made him think he was a grown-up Billy Goat and able to take care of himself. So one evening when the flock started home from the pasture and his mother called, the Kid paid no heed and kept right on nibbling the tender grass. A little later when he lifted his head, the flock was gone.

He was all alone. The sun was sinking. Long shadows came creeping over the ground. A chilly little wind came creeping with them making scary noises in the grass. The Kid shivered as he thought of the terrible Wolf. Then he started wildly over the field, bleating for his mother. But not half-way, near a clump of trees, there was the Wolf!

The Kid knew there was little hope for him.

"Please, Mr. Wolf," he said trembling, "I know you are going to eat me. But first please pipe me a tune, for I want to dance and be merry as long as I can."

The Wolf liked the idea of a little music before eating, so he struck up a merry tune and the Kid leaped and frisked gaily.

Meanwhile, the flock was moving slowly homeward. In the still evening air the Wolf's piping carried far. The Shepherd Dogs pricked up their ears. They recognized the song the Wolf sings before a feast, and in a moment they were racing back to the pasture. The Wolf's song ended suddenly, and as he ran, with the Dogs at his heels, he called himself a fool for turning piper to please a Kid, when he should have stuck to his butcher's trade.

Do not let anything turn you from your purpose.

THE TORTOISE AND
THE DUCKS

The Tortoise, you know, carries his house on his back. No matter how hard he tries, he cannot leave home. They say that Jupiter punished him so, because he was such a lazy stay-at-home that he would not go to Jupiter's wedding, even when especially invited.

After many years, Tortoise began to wish he had gone to that wedding. When he saw how gaily the birds flew about and how the Hare and the Chipmunk and all the other animals ran nimbly by, always eager to see everything there was to be seen, the Tortoise felt very sad and discontented. He wanted to see the world too, and there he was with a house on his back and little short legs that could hardly drag him along.

One day he met a pair of Ducks and told them all his trouble.

"We can help you to see the world," said the Ducks. "Take hold of this stick with your teeth and we will carry you far up in the air where you can see the whole countryside. But keep quiet or you will be sorry."

The Tortoise was very glad indeed. He seized the stick firmly with his teeth, the two Ducks took hold of it one at each end, and away they sailed up toward the clouds.

Just then a Crow flew by. He was very much astonished at the strange sight and cried:

"This must surely be the King of Tortoises!"

"Why certainly—" began the Tortoise.

But as he opened his mouth to say these foolish words he lost his hold on the stick, and down he fell to the ground, where he was dashed to pieces on a rock.

Foolish curiosity and vanity often lead to misfortune.

THE YOUNG CRAB AND HIS MOTHER

"Why in the world do you walk sideways like that?" said a Mother Crab to her son. "You should always walk straight forward with your toes turned out."

"Show me how to walk, mother dear," answered the little Crab obediently, "I want to learn."

So the old Crab tried and *tried* to walk straight forward. But she could walk sideways only, like her son. And when she wanted to turn her toes out she tripped and fell on her nose.

Do not tell others how to act unless you can set a good example.

THE FROGS AND THE OX

An Ox came down to a reedy pool to drink. As he splashed heavily into the water, he crushed a young Frog into the mud. The old Frog soon missed the little one and asked his brothers and sisters what had become of him.

"A *great big* monster," said one of them, "stepped on little brother with one of his huge feet!"

"Big, was he!" said the old Frog, puffing herself up. "Was he as big as this?"

"Oh, *much* bigger!" they cried.

The Frog puffed up still more.

"He could not have been bigger than this," she said. But the little Frogs all declared that the monster was *much*, *much* bigger and the old Frog kept puffing herself out more and more until, all at once, she burst.

Do not attempt the impossible.

THE DOG, THE COCK, AND THE FOX

A Dog and a Cock, who were the best of friends, wished very much to see something of the world. So they decided to leave the farmyard and to set out into the world along the road that led to the woods. The two comrades traveled along in the very best of spirits and without meeting any adventure to speak of.

At nightfall the Cock, looking for a place to roost, as was his custom, spied nearby a hollow tree that he thought would do very nicely for a night's lodging. The Dog could creep inside and the Cock would fly up on one of the branches. So said, so done, and both slept very comfortably.

With the first glimmer of dawn the Cock awoke. For the moment he forgot just where he was. He thought he was still in the farmyard where it had been his duty to arouse the household at daybreak. So standing on tip-toes he flapped his wings and crowed lustily. But instead of awakening the farmer, he awakened a Fox not far off in the wood. The Fox immediately had rosy visions of a very delicious breakfast. Hurrying to the tree where the Cock was roosting, he said very politely:

"A hearty welcome to our woods, honored sir. I cannot tell you how glad I am to see you here. I am quite sure we shall become the closest of friends."

"I feel highly flattered, kind sir," replied the Cock slyly. "If you will please go around to the door of my house at the foot of the tree, my porter will let you in."

The hungry but unsuspecting Fox, went around the tree as he was told, and in a twinkling the Dog had seized him.

Those who try to deceive may expect to be paid in their own coin.

BELLING THE CAT

The Mice once called a meeting to decide on a plan to free themselves of their enemy, the Cat. At least they wished to find some way of knowing when she was coming, so they might have time to run away. Indeed, something had to be done, for they lived in such constant fear of her claws that they hardly dared stir from their dens by night or day.

Many plans were discussed, but none of them was thought good enough. At last a very young Mouse got up and said:

"I have a plan that seems very simple, but I know it will be successful. All we have to do is to hang a bell about the Cat's neck. When we hear the bell ringing we will know immediately that our enemy is coming."

All the Mice were much surprised that they had not thought of such a plan before. But in the midst of the rejoicing over their good fortune, an old Mouse arose and said:

"I will say that the plan of the young Mouse is very good. But let me ask one question: Who will bell the Cat?"

It is one thing to say that something should be done, but quite a different matter to do it.

THE EAGLE AND THE JACKDAW

An Eagle, swooping down on powerful wings, seized a lamb in her talons and made off with it to her nest. A Jackdaw saw the deed, and his silly head was filled with the idea that he was big and strong enough to do as the Eagle had done. So with much rustling of feathers and a fierce air, he came down swiftly on the back of a large Ram. But when he tried to rise again he found that he could not get away, for his claws were tangled in the wool. And so far was he from carrying away the Ram, that the Ram hardly noticed he was there.

The Shepherd saw the fluttering Jackdaw and at once guessed what had happened. Running up, he caught the bird and clipped its wings. That evening he gave the Jackdaw to his children.

"What a funny bird this is!" they said laughing, "what do you call it, father?"

"That is a Jackdaw, my children. But if you should ask him, *he* would say he is an Eagle."

Do not let your vanity make you overestimate your powers.

THE BOY AND THE FILBERTS

A Boy was given permission to put his hand into a pitcher to get some filberts. But he took such a great fistful that he could not draw his hand out again. There he stood, unwilling to give up a single filbert and yet unable to get them all out at once. Vexed and disappointed he began to cry.

"My boy," said his mother, "be satisfied with half the nuts you have taken and you will easily get your hand out. Then perhaps you may have some more filberts some other time."

Do not attempt too much at once.

HERCULES AND THE WAGONER

A Farmer was driving his wagon along a miry country road after a heavy rain. The horses could hardly drag the load through the deep mud, and at last came to a standstill when one of the wheels sank to the hub in a rut.

The farmer climbed down from his seat and stood beside the wagon looking at it but without making the least effort to get it out of the rut. All he did was to curse his bad luck and call loudly on Hercules to come to his aid. Then, it is said, Hercules really did appear, saying:

"Put your shoulder to the wheel, man, and urge on your horses. Do you think you can move the wagon by simply looking at it and whining about it? Hercules will not help unless you make some effort to help yourself."

And when the farmer put his shoulder to the wheel and urged on the horses, the wagon moved very readily, and soon the Farmer was riding along in great content and with a good lesson learned.

Self help is the best help.

Heaven helps those who help themselves.

THE KID AND THE WOLF

A frisky young Kid had been left by the herdsman on the thatched roof of a sheep shelter to keep him out of harm's way. The Kid was browsing near the edge of the roof, when he spied a Wolf and began to jeer at him, making faces and abusing him to his heart's content.

"I hear you," said the Wolf, "and I haven't the least grudge against you for what you say or do. When you are up there it is the roof that's talking, not you."

Do not say anything at any time that you would not say at all times.

THE TOWN MOUSE AND THE COUNTRY MOUSE

A Town Mouse once visited a relative who lived in the country. For lunch the Country Mouse served wheat stalks, roots, and acorns, with a dash of cold water for drink. The Town Mouse ate very sparingly, nibbling a little of this and a little of that, and by her manner making it very plain that she ate the simple food only to be polite.

After the meal the friends had a long talk, or rather the Town Mouse talked about her life in the city while the Country Mouse listened. They then went to bed in a cozy nest in the hedgerow and slept in quiet and comfort until morning. In her sleep the Country Mouse dreamed she was a Town Mouse with all the luxuries and delights of city life that her friend had described for her. So the next day when the Town Mouse asked the Country Mouse to go home with her to the city, she gladly said yes.

When they reached the mansion in which the Town Mouse lived, they found on the table in the dining room the leavings of a very fine banquet. There were sweetmeats and jellies, pastries, delicious cheeses, indeed, the most tempting foods that a Mouse can imagine. But just as the Country Mouse was about to nibble a dainty bit of pastry, she heard a Cat mew loudly and scratch at the door. In great fear the Mice scurried to a hiding place, where they lay quite still for a long time, hardly daring to breathe. When at last they ventured back to the feast, the door opened suddenly and in came the servants to clear the table, followed by the House Dog.

The Country Mouse stopped in the Town Mouse's den only long enough to pick up her carpet bag and umbrella.

"You may have luxuries and dainties that I have not," she said as she hurried away, "but I prefer my plain food and simple life in the country with the peace and security that go with it."

Poverty with security is better than plenty in the midst of fear and uncertainty.

THE TOWN MOUSE AND THE COUNTRY MOUSE

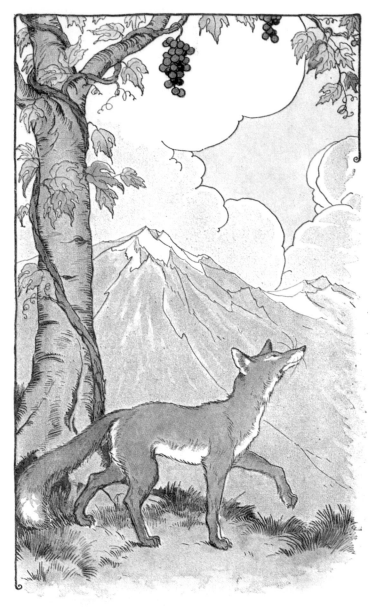

THE FOX AND THE GRAPES

A Fox one day spied a beautiful bunch of ripe grapes hanging from a vine trained along the branches of a tree. The grapes seemed ready to burst with juice, and the Fox's mouth watered as he gazed longingly at them.

The bunch hung from a high branch, and the Fox had to jump for it. The first time he jumped he missed it by a long way. So he walked off a short distance and took a running leap at it, only to fall short once more. Again and again he tried, but in vain.

Now he sat down and looked at the grapes in disgust.

"What a fool I am," he said. "Here I am wearing myself out to get a bunch of sour grapes that are not worth gaping for."

And off he walked very, very scornfully.

There are many who pretend to despise and belittle that which is beyond their reach.

THE BUNDLE OF STICKS

A certain Father had a family of Sons, who were forever quarreling among themselves. No words he could say did the least good, so he cast about in his mind for some very striking example that should make them see that discord would lead them to misfortune.

One day when the quarreling had been much more violent than usual and each of the Sons was moping in a surly manner, he asked one of them to bring him a bundle of sticks. Then handing the bundle to each of his Sons in turn he told them to try to break it. But although each one tried his best, none was able to do so.

The Father then untied the bundle and gave the sticks to his Sons to break one by one. This they did very easily.

"My Sons," said the Father, "do you not see how certain it is that if you agree with each other and help each other, it will be impossible for your enemies to injure you? But if you are divided among yourselves, you will be no stronger than a single stick in that bundle."

In unity is strength.

THE WOLF AND THE CRANE

A Wolf had been feasting too greedily, and a bone had stuck crosswise in his throat. He could get it neither up nor down, and of course he could not eat a thing. Naturally that was an awful state of affairs for a greedy Wolf.

So away he hurried to the Crane. He was sure that she, with her long neck and bill, would easily be able to reach the bone and pull it out.

"I will reward you very handsomely," said the Wolf, "if you pull that bone out for me."

The Crane, as you can imagine, was very uneasy about putting her head in a Wolf's throat. But she was grasping

in nature, so she did what the Wolf asked her to do.

When the Wolf felt that the bone was gone, he started to walk away.

"But what about my reward!" called the Crane anxiously.

"What!" snarled the Wolf, whirling around. "Haven't you got it? Isn't it enough that I let you take your head out of my mouth without snapping it off?"

Expect no reward for serving the wicked.

THE ASS AND HIS DRIVER

An Ass was being driven along a road leading down the mountain side, when he suddenly took it into his silly head to choose his own path. He could see his stall at the foot of the mountain, and to him the quickest way down seemed to be over the edge of the nearest cliff. Just as he was about to leap over, his master caught him by the tail and tried to pull him back, but the stubborn Ass would not yield and pulled with all his might.

"Very well," said his master, "go your way, you willful beast, and see where it leads you."

With that he let go, and the foolish Ass tumbled head over heels down the mountain side.

They who will not listen to reason but stubbornly go their own way against the friendly advice of those who are wiser than they, are on the road to misfortune.

THE OXEN AND THE WHEELS

A pair of Oxen were drawing a heavily loaded wagon along a miry country road. They had to use all their strength to pull the wagon, but they did not complain.

The Wheels of the wagon were of a different sort. Though the task they had to do was very light compared with that of the Oxen, they creaked and groaned at every turn. The poor Oxen, pulling with all their might to draw the wagon through the deep mud, had their ears filled with the loud complaining of the Wheels. And this, you may well know, made their work so much the harder to endure.

"Silence!" the Oxen cried at last, out of patience. "What have you Wheels to complain about so loudly? We are drawing all the weight, not you, and we are keeping still about it besides."

They complain most who suffer least.

THE LION AND THE MOUSE

A Lion lay asleep in the forest, his great head resting on his paws. A timid little Mouse came upon him unexpectedly, and in her fright and haste to get away, ran across the Lion's nose. Roused from his nap, the Lion laid his huge paw angrily on the tiny creature to kill her.

"Spare me!" begged the poor Mouse. "Please let me go and some day I will surely repay you."

The Lion was much amused to think that a Mouse could ever help him. But he was generous and finally let the Mouse go.

Some days later, while stalking his prey in the forest, the Lion was caught in the toils of a hunter's net. Unable to free himself, he filled the forest with his angry roaring. The Mouse knew the voice and quickly found the Lion struggling in the net. Running to one of the great ropes that bound him, she gnawed it until it parted, and soon the Lion was free.

"You laughed when I said I would repay you," said the Mouse. "Now you see that even a Mouse can help a Lion."

A kindness is never wasted.

THE SHEPHERD BOY AND THE WOLF

A Shepherd Boy tended his master's Sheep near a dark forest not far from the village. Soon he found life in the pasture very dull. All he could do to amuse himself was to talk to his dog or play on his shepherd's pipe.

One day as he sat watching the Sheep and the quiet forest, and thinking what he would do should he see a Wolf, he thought of a plan to amuse himself.

His Master had told him to call for help should a Wolf attack the flock, and the Villagers would drive it away. So now, though he had not seen anything that even looked like a Wolf, he ran toward the village shouting at the top of his voice, "Wolf! Wolf!"

As he expected, the Villagers who heard the cry dropped their work and ran in great excitement to the pasture. But when they got there they found the Boy doubled up with laughter at the trick he had played on them.

A few days later the Shepherd Boy again shouted, "Wolf! Wolf!" Again the Villagers ran to help him, only to be laughed at again.

Then one evening as the sun was setting behind the forest and the shadows were creeping out over the pasture, a Wolf really did spring from the underbrush and fall upon the Sheep.

In terror the Boy ran toward the village shouting "Wolf! Wolf!" But though the Villagers heard the cry, they did not run to help him as they had before. "He cannot fool us again," they said.

The Wolf killed a great many of the Boy's sheep and then slipped away into the forest.

Liars are not believed even when they speak the truth.

THE GNAT AND THE BULL

A Gnat flew over the meadow with much buzzing for so small a creature and settled on the tip of one of the horns of a Bull. After he had rested a short time, he made ready to fly away. But before he left he begged the Bull's pardon for having used his horn for a resting place.

"You must be very glad to have me go now," he said.

"It's all the same to me," replied the Bull. "I did not even know you were there."

We are often of greater importance in our own eyes than in the eyes of our neighbor.

The smaller the mind the greater the conceit.

THE PLANE TREE

Two Travellers, walking in the noonday sun, sought the shade of a widespreading tree to rest. As they lay looking up among the pleasant leaves, they saw that it was a Plane Tree.

"How useless is the Plane!" said one of them. "It bears no fruit whatever, and only serves to litter the ground with leaves."

"Ungrateful creatures!" said a voice from the Plane Tree. "You lie here in my cooling shade, and yet you say I am useless! Thus ungratefully, O Jupiter, do men receive their blessings!"

Our best blessings are often the least appreciated.

THE FARMER AND THE STORK

A Stork of a very simple and trusting nature had been asked by a gay party of Cranes to visit a field that had been newly planted. But the party ended dismally with all the birds entangled in the meshes of the Farmer's net.

The Stork begged the Farmer to spare him.

"Please let me go," he pleaded. "I belong to the Stork family who you know are honest and birds of good character. Besides, I did not know the Cranes were going to steal."

"You may be a very good bird," answered the Farmer, "but I caught you with the thieving Cranes and you will have to share the same punishment with them."

You are judged by the company you keep.

THE SHEEP AND THE PIG

One day a shepherd discovered a fat Pig in the meadow where his Sheep were pastured. He very quickly captured the porker, which squealed at the top of its voice the moment the Shepherd laid his hands on it. You would have thought, to hear the loud squealing, that the Pig was being cruelly hurt. But in spite of its squeals and struggles to escape, the Shepherd tucked his prize under his arm and started off to the butcher's in the market place.

The Sheep in the pasture were much astonished and amused at the Pig's behavior, and followed the Shepherd and his charge to the pasture gate.

"What makes you squeal like that?" asked one of the Sheep. "The Shepherd often catches and carries off one of us. But we should feel very much ashamed to make such a terrible fuss about it like you do."

"That is all very well," replied the Pig, with a squeal and a frantic kick. "When he catches you he is only after your wool. But he wants my bacon! gree-ee-ee!"

It is easy to be brave when there is no danger.

THE SHEEP AND THE PIG

THE TRAVELERS AND THE PURSE

Two men were traveling in company along the road when one of them picked up a well-filled purse.

"How lucky I am!" he said. "I have found a purse. Judging by its weight it must be full of gold."

"Do not say '*I* have found a purse,'" said his companion. "Say rather '*we* have found a purse' and 'how lucky *we* are.' Travelers ought to share alike the fortunes or misfortunes of the road."

"No, no," replied the other angrily. "*I* found it and *I* am going to keep it."

Just then they heard a shout of "Stop, thief!" and looking around, saw a mob of people armed with clubs coming down the road.

The man who had found the purse fell into a panic.

"We are lost if they find the purse on us," he cried.

"No, no," replied the other, "You would not say 'we' before, so now stick to your 'I'. Say '*I* am lost.'"

We cannot expect any one to share our misfortunes unless we are willing to share our good fortune also.

THE LION AND THE ASS

One day as the Lion walked proudly down a forest aisle, and the animals respectfully made way for him, an Ass brayed a scornful remark as he passed.

The Lion felt a flash of anger. But when he turned his head and saw who had spoken, he walked quietly on. He would not honor the fool with even so much as a stroke of his claws.

Do not resent the remarks of a fool. Ignore them.

THE FROGS WHO WISHED FOR A KING

The Frogs were tired of governing themselves. They had so much freedom that it had spoiled them, and they did nothing but sit around croaking in a bored manner and wishing for a government that could entertain them with the pomp and display of royalty, and rule them in a way to make them know they were being ruled. No milk and water government for them, they declared. So they sent a petition to Jupiter asking for a king.

Jupiter saw what simple and foolish creatures they were, but to keep them quiet and make them think they had a king he threw down a huge log, which fell into the water with a great splash. The Frogs hid themselves among the reeds and grasses, thinking the new king to be some fearful giant. But they soon discovered how tame and peaceable King Log was. In a short time the younger Frogs were using him for a diving platform, while the older Frogs made him a meeting place, where they complained loudly to Jupiter about the government.

To teach the Frogs a lesson the ruler of the gods now sent a

Crane to be king of Frogland. The Crane proved to be a very different sort of king from old King Log. He gobbled up the poor Frogs right and left and they soon saw what fools they had been. In mournful croaks they begged Jupiter to take away the cruel tyrant before they should all be destroyed.

"How now!" cried Jupiter "Are you not yet content? You have what you asked for and so you have only yourselves to blame for your misfortunes."

Be sure you can better your condition before you seek to change.

THE OWL AND THE GRASSHOPPER

The Owl always takes her sleep during the day. Then after sundown, when the rosy light fades from the sky and the shadows rise slowly through the wood, out she comes ruffling and blinking from the old hollow tree. Now her weird "hoo-hoo-hoo-oo-oo" echoes through the quiet wood, and she begins her hunt for the bugs and beetles, frogs and mice she likes so well to eat.

Now there was a certain old Owl who had become very cross and hard to please as she grew older, especially if anything disturbed her daily slumbers. One warm summer afternoon as she dozed away in her den in the old oak tree, a Grasshopper nearby began a joyous but very raspy song. Out popped the old Owl's head from the opening in the tree that served her both for door and for window.

"Get away from here, sir," she said to the Grasshopper. "Have you no manners? You should at least respect my age and leave me to sleep in quiet!"

But the Grasshopper answered saucily that he had as much right to his place in the sun as the Owl had to her place in the old oak.

Then he struck up a louder and still more rasping tune.

The wise old Owl knew quite well that it would do no good to argue with the Grasshopper, nor with anybody else for that matter. Besides, her eyes were not sharp enough by day to permit her to punish the Grasshopper as he deserved. So she laid aside all hard words and spoke very kindly to him.

"Well sir," she said, "if I must stay awake, I am going to settle right down to enjoy your singing. Now that I think of it, I have a wonderful wine here, sent me from Olympus, of which I am told Apollo drinks before he sings to the high gods. Please come up and taste this delicious drink with me. I know it will make you sing like Apollo himself."

The foolish Grasshopper was taken in by the Owl's flattering words. Up he jumped to the Owl's den, but as soon as he was near enough so the old Owl could see him clearly, she pounced upon him and ate him up.

Flattery is not a proof of true admiration.

Do not let flattery throw you off your guard against an enemy.

THE WOLF AND HIS SHADOW

A Wolf left his lair one evening in fine spirits and an excellent appetite. As he ran, the setting sun cast his shadow far out on the ground, and it looked as if the wolf were a hundred times bigger than he really was.

"Why," exclaimed the Wolf proudly, "see how big I am! Fancy *me* running away from a puny Lion! I'll show him who is fit to be king, he or I."

Just then an immense shadow blotted him out entirely, and the next instant a Lion struck him down with a single blow.

Do not let your fancy make you forget realities.

THE OAK AND THE REEDS

A Giant Oak stood near a brook in which grew some slender Reeds. When the wind blew, the great Oak stood proudly upright with its hundred arms uplifted to the sky. But the Reeds bowed low in the wind and sang a sad and mournful song.

"You have reason to complain," said the Oak. "The slightest breeze that ruffles the surface of the water makes you bow your heads, while I, the mighty Oak, stand upright and firm before the howling tempest."

"Do not worry about us," replied the Reeds. "The winds do not harm us. We bow before them and so we do not break. You, in all your pride and strength, have so far resisted their blows. But the end is coming."

As the Reeds spoke a great hurricane rushed out of the north. The Oak stood proudly and fought against the storm, while the yielding Reeds bowed low. The wind redoubled in fury, and all at once the great tree fell, torn up by the roots, and lay among the pitying Reeds.

Better to yield when it is folly to resist, than to resist stubbornly and be destroyed.

THE RAT AND THE ELEPHANT

A Rat was traveling along the King's highway. He was a very proud Rat, considering his small size and the bad reputation all Rats have. As Mr. Rat walked along—he kept mostly to the ditch—he noticed a great commotion up the road, and soon a grand procession came in view. It was the King and his retinue.

The King rode on a huge Elephant adorned with the most gorgeous trappings. With the King in his luxurious howdah were the royal Dog and Cat. A great crowd of people followed the procession. They were so taken up with admiration of the Elephant, that the Rat was not noticed. His pride was hurt.

"What fools!" he cried. "Look at me, and you will soon forget that clumsy Elephant! Is it his great size that makes your eyes pop out? Or is it his wrinkled hide? Why, I have eyes and ears and as many legs as he! I am of just as much importance, and"—

But just then the royal Cat spied him, and the next instant, the Rat knew he was *not* quite so important as an Elephant.

A resemblance to the great in some things does not make us great.

THE BOYS AND THE FROGS

Some Boys were playing one day at the edge of a pond in which lived a family of Frogs. The Boys amused themselves by throwing stones into the pond so as to make them skip on top of the water.

The stones were flying thick and fast and the Boys were enjoying themselves very much; but the poor Frogs in the pond were trembling with fear.

At last one of the Frogs, the oldest and bravest, put his head out of the water, and said, "Oh, please, dear children, stop your cruel play! Though it may be fun for you, it means death to us!"

Always stop to think whether your fun may not be the cause of another's unhappiness.

THE CROW AND THE PITCHER

In a spell of dry weather, when the Birds could find very little to drink, a thirsty Crow found a pitcher with a little water in it. But the pitcher was high and had a narrow neck, and no matter how he tried, the Crow could not reach the water. The poor thing felt as if he must die of thirst.

Then an idea came to him. Picking up some small pebbles, he dropped them into the pitcher one by one. With each pebble the water rose a little higher until at last it was near enough so he could drink.

In a pinch a good use of our wits may help us out.

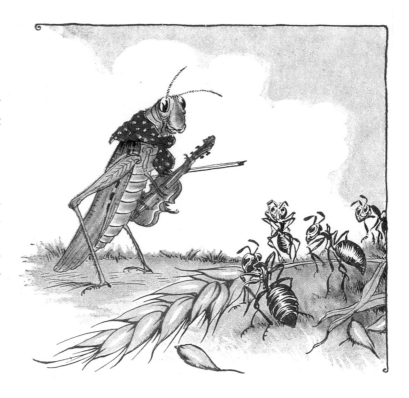

THE ANTS AND THE GRASSHOPPER

One bright day in late autumn a family of Ants were bustling about in the warm sunshine, drying out the grain they had stored up during the summer, when a starving Grasshopper, his fiddle under his arm, came up and humbly begged for a bite to eat.

"What!" cried the Ants in surprise, "haven't you stored anything away for the winter? What in the world were you doing all last summer?"

"I didn't have time to store up any food," whined the Grasshopper; "I was so busy making music that before I knew it the summer was gone."

The Ants shrugged their shoulders in disgust.

"Making music, were you?" they cried. "Very well; now dance!" And they turned their backs on the Grasshopper and went on with their work.

There's a time for work and a time for play.

THE ASS CARRYING THE IMAGE

A sacred Image was being carried to the temple. It was mounted on an Ass adorned with garlands and gorgeous trappings, and a grand procession of priests and pages followed it through the streets. As the Ass walked along, the people bowed their heads reverently or fell on their knees, and the Ass thought the honor was being paid to himself.

With his head full of this foolish idea, he became so puffed up with pride and vanity that he halted and started to bray loudly. But in the midst of his song, his driver guessed what the Ass had got into his head, and began to beat him unmercifully with a stick.

"Go along with you, you stupid Ass," he cried. "The honor is not meant for you but for the image you are carrying."

Do not try to take the credit to yourself that is due to others.

A RAVEN AND A SWAN

A Raven, which you know is black as coal, was envious of the Swan, because her feathers were as white as the purest snow. The foolish bird got the idea that if he lived like the Swan, swimming and diving all day long and eating the weeds and plants that grow in the water, his feathers would turn white like the Swan's.

So he left his home in the woods and fields and flew down to live on the lakes and in the marshes. But though he washed and washed all day long, almost drowning himself at it, his feathers remained as black as ever. And as the water weeds he ate did not agree with him, he got thinner and thinner, and at last he died.

A change of habits will not alter nature.

THE TWO GOATS

Two Goats, frisking gayly on the rocky steeps of a mountain valley, chanced to meet, one on each side of a deep chasm through which poured a mighty mountain torrent. The trunk of a fallen tree formed the only means of crossing the chasm, and on this not even two squirrels could have passed each other in safety. The narrow path would have made the bravest tremble. Not so our Goats. Their pride would not permit either to stand aside for the other.

One set her foot on the log. The other did likewise. In the middle they met horn to horn. Neither would give way, and so they both fell, to be swept away by the roaring torrent below.

It is better to yield than to come to misfortune through stubbornness.

THE ASS AND THE LOAD OF SALT

A Merchant, driving his Ass homeward from the seashore with a heavy load of salt, came to a river crossed by a shallow ford. They had crossed this river many times before without accident, but this time the Ass slipped and fell when halfway over. And when the Merchant at last got him to his feet, much of the salt had melted away. Delighted to find how much lighter his burden had become, the Ass finished the journey very gayly.

Next day the Merchant went for another load of salt. On the way home the Ass, remembering what had happened at the ford, purposely let himself fall into the water, and again got rid of most of his burden.

The angry Merchant immediately turned about and drove the Ass back to the seashore, where he loaded him with two great baskets of sponges. At the ford the Ass again tumbled over; but when he had scrambled to his feet, it was a very disconsolate Ass that dragged himself homeward under a load ten times heavier than before.

The same measures will not suit all circumstances.

THE ASS AND THE LOAD OF SALT

THE LION AND THE GNAT

"Away with you, vile insect!" said a Lion angrily to a Gnat that was buzzing around his head. But the Gnat was not in the least disturbed.

"Do you think," he said spitefully to the Lion, "that I am afraid of you because they call you king?"

The next instant he flew at the Lion and stung him sharply on the nose. Mad with rage, the Lion struck fiercely at the Gnat, but only succeeded in tearing himself with his claws. Again and again the Gnat stung the Lion, who now was roaring terribly. At last, worn out with rage and covered with wounds that his own teeth and claws had made, the Lion gave up the fight.

The Gnat buzzed away to tell the whole world about his victory, but instead he flew straight into a spider's web. And there, he who had defeated the King of beasts came to a miserable end, the prey of a little spider.

The least of our enemies is often the most to be feared.

Pride over a success should not throw us off our guard.

THE LEAP AT RHODES

A certain man who visited foreign lands could talk of little when he returned to his home except the wonderful adventures he had met with and the great deeds he had done abroad.

One of the feats he told about was a leap he had made in a city called Rhodes. That leap was so great, he said, that no other man could leap anywhere near the distance. A great many persons in Rhodes had seen him do it and would prove that what he told was true.

"No need of witnesses," said one of the hearers. "Suppose this city is Rhodes. Now show us how far you can jump."

Deeds count, not boasting words.

THE COCK AND THE JEWEL

A Cock was busily scratching and scraping about to find something to eat for himself and his family, when he happened to turn up a precious jewel that had been lost by its owner.

"Aha!" said the Cock. "No doubt you are very costly and he who lost you would give a great deal to find you. But as for me, I would choose a single grain of barleycorn before all the jewels in the world."

Precious things are without value to those who cannot prize them.

THE MONKEY AND THE CAMEL

At a great celebration in honor of King Lion, the Monkey was asked to dance for the company. His dancing was very clever indeed, and the animals were all highly pleased with his grace and lightness.

The praise that was showered on the Monkey made the Camel envious. He was very sure that he could dance quite as well as the Monkey, if not better, so he pushed his way into the crowd that was gathered around the Monkey, and rising on his hind legs, began to dance. But the big hulking Camel made himself very ridiculous as he kicked out his knotty legs and twisted his long clumsy neck. Besides, the animals found it hard to keep their toes from under his heavy hoofs.

At last, when one of his huge feet came within an inch of King Lion's nose, the animals were so disgusted that they set upon the Camel in a rage and drove him out into the desert.

Shortly afterward, refreshments, consisting mostly of Camel's hump and ribs, were served to the company.

Do not try to ape your betters.

THE WILD BOAR AND THE FOX

A Wild Boar was sharpening his tusks busily against the stump of a tree, when a Fox happened by. Now the Fox was always looking for a chance to make fun of his neighbors. So he made a great show of looking anxiously about, as if in fear of some hidden enemy. But the Boar kept right on with his work.

"Why are you doing that?" asked the Fox at last with a grin. "There isn't any danger that I can see."

"True enough," replied the Boar, "but when danger does come there will not be time for such work as this. My weapons will have to be ready for use then, or I shall suffer for it."

Preparedness for war is the best guarantee of peace.

THE ASS, THE FOX, AND THE LION

An Ass and a Fox had become close comrades, and were constantly in each other's company. While the Ass cropped a fresh bit of greens, the Fox would devour a chicken from the neighboring farmyard or a bit of cheese filched from the dairy. One day the pair unexpectedly met a Lion. The Ass was very much frightened, but the Fox calmed his fears.

"I will talk to him," he said.

So the Fox walked boldly up to the Lion.

"Your highness," he said in an undertone, so the Ass could not hear him, "I've got a fine scheme in my head. If you promise not to hurt me, I will lead that foolish creature yonder into a pit where he can't get out, and you can feast at your pleasure."

The Lion agreed and the Fox returned to the Ass.

"I made him promise not to hurt us," said the Fox. "But come, I know a good place to hide till he is gone."

So the Fox led the Ass into a deep pit. But when the Lion saw that the Ass was his for the taking, he first of all struck down the traitor Fox.

Traitors may expect treachery.

THE BIRDS, THE BEASTS, AND THE BAT

The Birds and the Beasts declared war against each other. No compromise was possible, and so they went at it tooth and claw. It is said the quarrel grew out of the persecution the race of Geese suffered at the teeth of the Fox family. The Beasts, too, had cause for fight. The Eagle was constantly pouncing on the Hare, and the Owl dined daily on Mice.

It was a terrible battle. Many a Hare and many a Mouse died. Chickens and Geese fell by the score—and the victor always stopped for a feast.

Now the Bat family had not openly joined either side. They were a very politic race. So when they saw the Birds getting the better of it, they were Birds for all there was in it. But when the tide of battle turned, they immediately sided with the Beasts.

When the battle was over, the conduct of the Bats was discussed at the peace conference. Such deceit was unpardonable, and Birds and Beasts made common cause to drive out the Bats. And since then the Bat family hides in dark towers and deserted ruins, flying out only in the night.

The deceitful have no friends.

THE LION, THE BEAR, AND THE FOX

Just as a great Bear rushed to seize a stray kid, a Lion leaped from another direction upon the same prey. The two fought furiously for the prize until they had received so many wounds that both sank down unable to continue the battle.

Just then a Fox dashed up, and seizing the kid, made off with it as fast as he could go, while the Lion and the Bear looked on in helpless rage.

"How much better it would have been," they said, "to have shared in a friendly spirit."

Those who have all the toil do not always get the profit.

THE WOLF AND THE LAMB

A stray Lamb stood drinking early one morning on the bank of a woodland stream. That very same morning a hungry Wolf came by farther up the stream, hunting for something to eat. He soon got his eyes on the Lamb. As a rule Mr. Wolf snapped up such delicious morsels without making any bones about it, but this Lamb looked so very helpless and innocent that the Wolf felt he ought to have some kind of an excuse for taking its life.

"How dare you paddle around in my stream and stir up all the mud!" he shouted fiercely. "You deserve to be punished severely for your rashness!"

"But, your highness," replied the trembling Lamb, "do not be angry! I cannot possibly muddy the water you are drinking up there. Remember, you are upstream and I am downstream."

"You *do* muddy it!" retorted the Wolf savagely. "And besides, I have heard that you told lies about me last year!"

"How could I have done so?" pleaded the Lamb. "I wasn't born until this year."

"If it wasn't you, it was your brother!"

"I have no brothers."

"Well, then," snarled the Wolf, "It was someone in your family anyway. But no matter who it was, I do not intend to be talked out of my breakfast."

And without more words the Wolf seized the poor Lamb and carried her off to the forest.

The tyrant can always find an excuse for his tyranny.

The unjust will not listen to the reasoning of the innocent.

THE WOLF AND THE SHEEP

A Wolf had been hurt in a fight with a Bear. He was unable to move and could not satisfy his hunger and thirst. A Sheep passed by near his hiding place, and the Wolf called to him,

"Please fetch me a drink of water," he begged; "that might give me strength enough so I can get me some solid food."

"Solid food!" said the Sheep. "That means me, I suppose. If I should bring you a drink, it would only serve to wash me down your throat. Don't talk to me about a drink!"

A knave's hypocrisy is easily seen through.

THE HARES AND THE FROGS

Hares, as you know, are very timid. The least shadow, sends them scurrying in fright to a hiding place. Once they decided to die rather than live in such misery. But while they were debating how best to meet death, they thought they heard a noise and in a flash were scampering off to the warren. On the way they passed a pond where a family of Frogs was sitting among the reeds on the bank. In an instant the startled Frogs were seeking safety in the mud.

"Look," cried a Hare, "things are not so bad after all, for here are creatures who are even afraid of us!"

However unfortunate we may think we are there is always someone worse off than ourselves.

very tip of his bill. Not a drop of soup could he get. But the Fox lapped it up easily, and, to increase the disappointment of the Stork, made a great show of enjoyment.

The hungry Stork was much displeased at the trick, but he was a calm, even-tempered fellow and saw no good in flying into a rage. Instead, not long afterward, he invited the Fox to dine with him in turn. The Fox arrived promptly at the time that had been set, and the Stork served a fish dinner that had a very appetizing smell. But it was

THE FOX AND THE STORK

The Fox one day thought of a plan to amuse himself at the expense of the Stork, at whose odd appearance he was always laughing.

"You must come and dine with me today," he said to the Stork, smiling to himself at the trick he was going to play. The Stork gladly accepted the invitation and arrived in good time and with a very good appetite.

For dinner the Fox served soup. But it was set out in a very shallow dish, and all the Stork could do was to wet the served in a tall jar with a very narrow neck. The Stork could easily get at the food with his long bill, but all the Fox could do was to lick the outside of the jar, and sniff at the delicious odor. And when the Fox lost his temper, the Stork said calmly:

Do not play tricks on your neighbors unless you can stand the same treatment yourself.

THE TRAVELERS AND THE SEA

Two Travelers were walking along the seashore. Far out they saw something riding on the waves.

"Look," said one, "a great ship rides in from distant lands, bearing rich treasures!"

The object they saw came ever nearer the shore.

"No," said the other, "that is not a treasure ship. That is some fisherman's skiff, with the day's catch of savoury fish."

Still nearer came the object. The waves washed it up on shore.

"It is a chest of gold lost from some wreck," they cried. Both Travelers rushed to the beach, but there they found nothing but a water-soaked log.

Do not let your hopes carry you away from reality.

THE WOLF AND THE LION

A Wolf had stolen a Lamb and was carrying it off to his lair to eat it. But his plans were very much changed when he met a Lion, who, without making any excuses, took the Lamb away from him.

The Wolf made off to a safe distance, and then said in a much injured tone:

"You have no right to take my property like that!"

The Lion looked back, but as the Wolf was too far away to be taught a lesson without too much inconvenience, he said:

"Your property? Did you buy it, or did the Shepherd make you a gift of it? Pray tell me, how did you get it?"

What is evil won is evil lost.

THE STAG AND HIS REFLECTION

A Stag, drinking from a crystal spring, saw himself mirrored in the clear water. He greatly admired the graceful arch of his antlers, but he was very much ashamed of his spindling legs.

"How can it be," he sighed, "that I should be cursed with such legs when I have so magnificent a crown."

At that moment he scented a panther and in an instant was bounding away through the forest. But as he ran his wide-spreading antlers caught in the branches of the trees, and soon the Panther overtook him. Then the Stag perceived that the legs of which he was so ashamed would have saved him had it not been for the useless ornaments on his head.

We often make much of the ornamental and despise the useful.

THE PEACOCK

The Peacock, they say, did not at first have the beautiful feathers in which he now takes so much pride. These, Juno, whose favorite he was, granted to him one day when he begged her for a train of feathers to distinguish him from the other birds. Then, decked in his finery, gleaming with emerald, gold, purple, and azure, he strutted proudly among the birds. All regarded him with envy. Even the most beautiful pheasant could see that his beauty was surpassed.

Presently the Peacock saw an Eagle soaring high up in the blue sky and felt a desire to fly, as he had been accustomed to do. Lifting his wings he tried to rise from the ground. But the weight of his magnificent train held him down. Instead of flying up to greet the first rays of the morning sun or to bathe in the rosy light among the floating clouds at sunset, he would have to walk the ground more encumbered and oppressed than any common barnyard fowl.

Do not sacrifice your freedom for the sake of pomp and show.

THE PEACOCK

THE LION AND THE ASS

A Lion and an Ass agreed to go hunting together. In their search for game the hunters saw a number of Wild Goats run into a cave, and laid plans to catch them. The Ass was to go into the cave and drive the Goats out, while the Lion would stand at the entrance to strike them down.

The plan worked beautifully. The Ass made such a frightful din in the cave, kicking and braying with all his might, that the Goats came running out in a panic of fear, only to fall victim to the Lion.

The Ass came proudly out of the cave.

"Did you see how I made them run?" he said.

"Yes, indeed," answered the Lion, "and if I had not known you and your kind I should certainly have run, too."

The loud-mouthed boaster does not impress nor frighten those who know him.

THE DOG AND HIS MASTER'S DINNER

A Dog had learned to carry his master's dinner to him every day. He was very faithful to his duty, though the smell of the good things in the basket tempted him.

The Dogs in the neighborhood noticed him carrying the basket and soon discovered what was in it. They made several attempts to steal it from him. But he always guarded it faithfully.

Then one day all the Dogs in the neighborhood got together and met him on his way with the basket. The Dog tried to run away from them. But at last he stopped to argue.

That was his mistake. They soon made him feel so ridiculous that he dropped the basket and seized a large piece of roast meat intended for his master's dinner.

"Very well," he said, "you divide the rest."

Do not stop to argue with temptation.

Dressed in his borrowed finery he strutted loftily among the birds of his own kind. Then he flew down into the garden among the Peacocks. But they soon saw who he was. Angry at the cheat, they flew at him, plucking away the borrowed feathers and also some of his own.

The poor Jackdaw returned sadly to his former companions. There another unpleasant surprise awaited him. They had not forgotten his superior airs toward them, and, to punish him, they drove him away with a rain of pecks and jeers.

Borrowed feathers do not make fine birds.

THE VAIN JACKDAW AND HIS BORROWED FEATHERS

A Jackdaw chanced to fly over the garden of the King's palace. There he saw with much wonder and envy a flock of royal Peacocks in all the glory of their splendid plumage.

Now the black Jackdaw was not a very handsome bird, nor very refined in manner. Yet he imagined that all he needed to make himself fit for the society of the Peacocks was a dress like theirs. So he picked up some castoff feathers of the Peacocks and stuck them among his own black plumes.

THE MONKEY AND
THE DOLPHIN

It happened once upon a time that a certain Greek ship bound for Athens was wrecked off the coast close to Piraeus, the port of Athens. Had it not been for the Dolphins, who at that time were very friendly toward mankind and especially toward Athenians, all would have perished. But the Dolphins took the ship-wrecked people on their backs and swam with them to shore.

Now it was the custom among the Greeks to take their pet monkeys and dogs with them whenever they went on a voyage. So when one of the Dolphins saw a Monkey struggling in the water, he thought it was a man, and made the Monkey climb up on his back. Then off he swam with him toward the shore.

The Monkey sat up, grave and dignified, on the Dolphin's back.

"You are a citizen of illustrious Athens, are you not?" asked the Dolphin politely.

"Yes," answered the Monkey, proudly. "My family is one of the noblest in the city."

"Indeed," said the Dolphin. "Then of course you often visit Piraeus."

"Yes, yes," replied the Monkey. "Indeed, I do. I am with him constantly. Piraeus is my very best friend."

This answer took the Dolphin by surprise, and, turning his head, he now saw what it was he was carrying. Without more ado, he dived and left the foolish Monkey to take care of himself, while he swam off in search of some human being to save.

One falsehood leads to another.

THE WOLF AND THE ASS

An Ass was feeding in a pasture near a wood when he saw a Wolf lurking in the shadows along the hedge. He easily guessed what the Wolf had in mind, and thought of a plan to save himself. So he pretended he was lame, and began to hobble painfully.

When the Wolf came up, he asked the Ass what had made him lame, and the Ass replied that he had stepped on a sharp thorn.

"Please pull it out," he pleaded, groaning as if in pain. "If you do not, it might stick in your throat when you eat me."

The Wolf saw the wisdom of the advice, for he wanted to enjoy his meal without any danger of choking. So the Ass lifted up his foot and the Wolf began to search very closely and carefully for the thorn.

Just then the Ass kicked out with all his might, tumbling the Wolf a dozen paces away. And while the Wolf was getting very slowly and painfully to his feet, the Ass galloped away in safety.

"Serves me right," growled the Wolf as he crept into the bushes. "I'm a butcher by trade, not a doctor."

Stick to your trade.

THE MONKEY AND THE CAT

Once upon a time a Cat and a Monkey lived as pets in the same house. They were great friends and were constantly in all sorts of mischief together. What they seemed to think of more than anything else was to get something to eat, and it did not matter much to them how they got it.

One day they were sitting by the fire, watching some chestnuts roasting on the hearth. How to get them was the question.

"I would gladly get them," said the cunning Monkey, "but you are much more skillful at such things than I am. Pull them out and I'll divide them between us."

Pussy stretched out her paw very carefully, pushed aside some of the cinders, and drew back her paw very quickly. Then she tried it again, this time pulling a chestnut half out of the fire. A third time and she drew out the chestnut. This performance she went through several times, each time singeing her paw severely. As fast as she pulled the chestnuts out of the fire, the Monkey ate them up.

Now the master came in, and away scampered the rascals, Mistress Cat with a burnt paw and no chestnuts. From that time on, they say, she contented herself with mice and rats and had little to do with Sir Monkey.

The flatterer seeks some benefit at your expense.

THE DOGS AND THE FOX

Some Dogs found the skin of a Lion and furiously began to tear it with their teeth. A Fox chanced to see them and laughed scornfully.

"If that Lion had been alive," he said, "it would have been a very different story. He would have made you feel how much sharper his claws are than your teeth."

It is easy and also contemptible to kick a man that is down.

THE DOGS AND THE HIDES

Some hungry Dogs saw a number of hides at the bottom of a stream where the Tanner had put them to soak. A fine hide makes an excellent meal for a hungry Dog, but the water was deep and the Dogs could not reach the hides from the bank. So they held a council and decided that the very best thing to do was to drink up the river.

All fell to lapping up the water as fast as they could. But though they drank and drank until, one after another, all of them had burst with drinking, still, for all their effort, the water in the river remained as high as ever.

Do not try to do impossible things.

THE RABBIT, THE WEASEL, AND THE CAT

A Rabbit left his home one day for a dinner of clover. But he forgot to latch the door of his house and while he was gone a Weasel walked in and calmly made himself at home. When the Rabbit returned, there was the Weasel's nose sticking out of the Rabbit's own doorway, sniffing the fine air.

The Rabbit was quite angry —for a Rabbit—, and requested

the Weasel to move out. But the Weasel was perfectly content. He was settled down for good.

A wise old Cat heard the dispute and offered to settle it.

"Come close to me," said the Cat, "I am very deaf. Put your mouths close to my ears while you tell me the facts."

The unsuspecting pair did as they were told and in an instant the Cat had them both under her claws. No one could deny that the dispute had been definitely settled.

The strong are apt to settle questions to their own advantage.

was able to save himself only by diving into a pool of water.

It is wiser to bear a single injury in silence than to provoke a thousand by flying into a rage.

THE FOX AND THE LEOPARD

A Fox and a Leopard, resting lazily after a generous dinner, amused themselves by disputing about their good looks. The Leopard was very proud of his glossy, spotted coat and made disdainful remarks about the Fox, whose appearance he declared was quite ordinary.

The Fox prided himself on his fine bushy tail with its tip of white, but he was wise enough to see that he could not rival the Leopard in looks. Still he kept up a flow of sarcastic talk, just to exercise his wits and to have the fun of disputing. The Leopard was about to lose his temper when the Fox got up, yawning lazily.

"You may have a very smart coat," he said, "but you would be a great deal better off if you had a little more smartness inside your head and less on your ribs, the way I am. That's what I call real beauty."

A fine coat is not always an indication of an attractive mind.

THE BEAR AND THE BEES

A Bear roaming the woods in search of berries happened on a fallen tree in which a swarm of Bees had stored their honey. The Bear began to nose around the log very carefully to find out if the Bees were at home. Just then one of the swarm came home from the clover field with a load of sweets. Guessing what the Bear was after, the Bee flew at him, stung him sharply and then disappeared into the hollow log.

The Bear lost his temper in an instant, and sprang upon the log tooth and claw, to destroy the nest. But this only brought out the whole swarm. The poor Bear had to take to his heels, and he

THE FOX AND THE LEOPARD

THE TWO POTS

Two Pots, one of brass and the other of clay, stood together on the hearthstone. One day the Brass Pot proposed to the Earthen Pot that they go out into the world together. But the Earthen Pot excused himself, saying that it would be wiser for him to stay in the corner by the fire.

"It would take so little to break me," he said. "You know how fragile I am. The least shock is sure to shatter me!"

"Don't let that keep you at home," urged the Brass Pot. "I shall take very good care of you. If we should happen to meet anything hard I will step between and save you."

So the Earthen Pot at last consented, and the two set out side by side, jolting along on three stubby legs first to this side, then to that, and bumping into each other at every step.

The Earthen Pot could not survive that sort of companionship very long. They had not gone ten paces before the Earthen Pot cracked, and at the next jolt he flew into a thousand pieces.

Equals make the best friends.

THE GOOSE AND THE GOLDEN EGG

There was once a Countryman who possessed the most wonderful Goose you can imagine, for every day when he visited the nest, the Goose had laid a beautiful, glittering, golden egg.

The Countryman took the eggs to market and soon began to get rich. But it was not long before he grew impatient with the Goose because she gave him only a single golden egg a day. He was not getting rich fast enough.

Then one day, after he had finished counting his money, the idea came to him that he could get all the golden eggs at once by killing the Goose and cutting it open. But when the deed was done, not a single golden egg did he find, and his precious Goose was dead.

Those who have plenty want more and so lose all they have.

THE GOOSE AND THE GOLDEN EGG

THE SPENDTHRIFT AND THE SWALLOW

A young fellow, who was very popular among his boon companions as a good spender, quickly wasted his fortune trying to live up to his reputation. Then one fine day in early spring he found himself with not a penny left, and no property save the clothes he wore.

He was to meet some jolly young men that morning, and he was at his wits' end how to get enough money to keep up appearances. Just then a Swallow flew by, twittering merrily, and the young man, thinking summer had come, hastened off to a clothes dealer, to whom he sold all the clothes he wore down to his very tunic.

A few days later a change in weather brought a severe frost; and the poor swallow and that foolish young man in his light tunic, and with his arms and knees bare, could scarely keep life in their shivering bodies.

One swallow does not make a summer.

THE CAT AND THE BIRDS

A Cat was growing very thin. As you have guessed, he did not get enough to eat. One day he heard that some Birds in the neighborhood were ailing and needed a doctor. So he put on a pair of spectacles, and with a leather box in his hand, knocked at the door of the Bird's home.

The Birds peeped out, and Dr. Cat, with much solicitude, asked how they were. He would be very happy to give them some medicine.

"Tweet, tweet," laughed the Birds. "Very smart, aren't you? We are very well, thank you, and more so, if *you* only keep away from here."

Be wise and shun the quack.

THE DOG AND THE OYSTER

There was once a Dog who was very fond of eggs. He visited the hen house very often and at last got so greedy that he would swallow the eggs whole.

One day the Dog wandered down to the seashore. There he spied an Oyster. In a twinkling the Oyster was resting in the Dog's stomach, shell and all.

It pained the Dog a good deal, as you can guess.

"I've learned that all round things are not eggs," he said groaning.

Act in haste and repent at leisure — and often in pain.

THE ASTROLOGER

A man who lived a long time ago believed that he could read the future in the stars. He called himself an Astrologer, and spent his time at night gazing at the sky.

One evening he was walking along the open road outside the village. His eyes were fixed on the stars. He thought he saw there that the end of the world was at hand, when all at once, down he went into a hole full of mud and water.

There he stood up to his ears, in the muddy water, and madly clawing at the slippery sides of the hole in his effort to climb out.

His cries for help soon brought the villagers running. As they pulled him out of the mud, one of them said:

"You pretend to read the future in the stars, and yet you fail to see what is at your feet! This may teach you to pay more attention to what is right in front of you, and let the future take care of itself."

"What use is it," said another, "to read the stars, when you can't see what's right here on the earth?"

Take care of the little things and the big things will take care of themselves.

THREE BULLOCKS AND A LION

A Lion had been watching three Bullocks feeding in an open field. He had tried to attack them several times, but they had kept together, and helped each other to drive him off. The Lion had little hope of eating them, for he was no match for three strong Bullocks with their sharp horns and hoofs. But he could not keep away from that field, for it is hard to resist watching a good meal, even when there is little chance of getting it.

Then one day the Bullocks had a quarrel, and when the hungry Lion came to look at them and lick his chops as he was accustomed to do, he found them in separate corners of the field, as far away from one another as they could get.

It was now an easy matter for the Lion to attack them one at a time, and this he proceeded to do with the greatest satisfaction and relish.

In unity is strength.

MERCURY AND THE WOODMAN

A poor Woodman was cutting down a tree near the edge of a deep pool in the forest. It was late in the day and the Woodman was tired. He had been working since sunrise and his strokes were not so sure as they had been early that morning. Thus it happened that the axe slipped and flew out of his hands into the pool.

The Woodman was in despair. The axe was all he possessed with which to make a living, and he had not money enough to buy a new one. As he stood wringing his hands and weeping, the god Mercury suddenly appeared and asked what the trouble was. The Woodman told what had happened, and straightway the kind Mercury dived into the pool. When he came up again he held a wonderful golden axe.

"Is this your axe?" Mercury asked the Woodman.

"No," answered the honest Woodman, "that is not my axe."

Mercury laid the golden axe on the bank and sprang back into the pool. This time he brought up an axe of silver, but the Woodman declared again that his axe was just an ordinary one with a wooden handle.

Mercury dived down for the third time, and when he came up again he had the very axe that had been lost.

The poor Woodman was very glad that his axe had been found and could not thank the kind god enough. Mercury was greatly pleased with the Woodman's honesty.

"I admire your honesty," he said, "and as a reward you may have all three axes, the gold and the silver as well as your own."

The happy Woodman returned to his home with his treasures, and soon the story of his good fortune was known to everybody in the village. Now there were several Woodmen in the village who believed that they could easily win the same good fortune. They hurried out into the woods, one here, one there, and hiding their axes in the bushes, pretended they had lost them. Then they wept and wailed and called on Mercury to help them.

And indeed, Mercury did appear, first to this one, then to that. To each one he showed an axe of gold, and each one eagerly claimed it to be the one he had lost. But Mercury did not give them the golden axe. Oh no! Instead he gave them each a hard whack over the head with it and sent them home. And when they returned next day to look for their own axes, they were nowhere to be found.

Honesty is the best policy.

THE FROG AND THE MOUSE

A young Mouse in search of adventure was running along the bank of a pond where lived a Frog. When the Frog saw the Mouse, he swam to the bank and croaked:

"Won't you pay me a visit? I can promise you a good time if you do."

The Mouse did not need much coaxing, for he was very anxious to see the world and everything in it. But though he could swim a little, he did not dare risk going into the pond without some help.

The Frog had a plan. He tied the Mouse's leg to his own with a tough reed. Then into the pond he jumped, dragging his foolish companion with him.

The Mouse soon had enough of it and wanted to return to shore; but the treacherous Frog had other plans. He pulled the Mouse down under the water and drowned him. But before he could untie the reed that bound him to the dead Mouse, a Hawk came sailing over the pond. Seeing the body of the Mouse floating on the water, the Hawk swooped down, seized the Mouse and carried it off, with the Frog dangling from its leg. Thus at one swoop he had caught both meat and fish for his dinner.

Those who seek to harm others often come to harm themselves through their own deceit.

THE FOX AND THE CRAB

A Crab one day grew disgusted with the sands in which he lived. He decided to take a stroll to the meadow not far inland. There he would find better fare than briny water and sand mites. So off he crawled to the meadow. But there a hungry Fox spied him, and in a twinkling, ate him up, both shell and claw.

Be content with your lot.

THE SERPENT AND THE EAGLE

A Serpent had succeeded in surprising an Eagle and had wrapped himself around the Eagle's neck. The Eagle could not reach the Serpent, neither with beak nor claws. Far into the sky he soared trying to shake off his enemy. But the Serpent's hold only tightened, and slowly the Eagle sank back to earth, gasping for breath.

A Countryman chanced to see the unequal combat. In pity for the noble Eagle he rushed up and soon had loosened the coiling Serpent and freed the Eagle.

The Serpent was furious. He had no chance to bite the watchful Countryman. Instead he struck at the drinking horn, hanging at the Countryman's belt, and into it let fly the poison of his fangs.

The Countryman now went on toward home. Becoming thirsty on the way, he filled his horn at a spring, and was about to drink. There was a sudden rush of great wings. Sweeping down, the Eagle seized the poisoned horn from out his savior's hands, and flew away with it to hide it where it could never be found.

An act of kindness is well repaid.

THE WOLF IN SHEEP'S CLOTHING

A certain Wolf could not get enough to eat because of the watchfulness of the Shepherds. But one night he found a sheep skin that had been cast aside and forgotten. The next day, dressed in the skin, the Wolf strolled into the pasture with the Sheep. Soon a little Lamb was following him about and was quickly led away to slaughter.

That evening the Wolf entered the fold with the flock. But it happened that the Shepherd took a fancy for mutton broth that very evening, and, picking up a knife, went to the fold. There the first he laid hands on and killed was the Wolf.

The evil doer often comes to harm through his own deceit.

THE BULL AND THE GOAT

A Bull once escaped from a Lion by entering a cave which the Goatherds used to house their flocks in stormy weather and at night. It happened that one of the Goats had been left behind, and the Bull had no sooner got inside than this Goat lowered his head and made a rush at him, butting him with his horns. As the Lion was still prowling outside the entrance to the cave, the Bull had to submit to the insult.

"Do not think," he said, "that I submit to your cowardly treatment because I am afraid of you. When that Lion leaves, I'll teach you a lesson you won't forget."

It is wicked to take advantage of another's distress.

THE EAGLE AND THE BEETLE

A Beetle once begged the Eagle to spare a Hare which had run to her for protection. But the Eagle pounced upon her prey, the sweep of her great wings tumbling the Beetle a dozen feet away. Furious at the disrespect shown her, the Beetle flew to the Eagle's nest and rolled out the eggs. Not one did she spare. The Eagle's grief and anger knew no bounds, but who had done the cruel deed she did not know.

Next year the Eagle built her nest far up on a mountain crag; but the Beetle found it and again destroyed the eggs. In despair the Eagle now implored great Jupiter to let her place her eggs in his lap. There none would dare harm them. But the Beetle buzzed about Jupiter's head, and made him rise to drive her away; and the eggs rolled from his lap.

Now the Beetle told the reason for her action, and Jupiter had to acknowledge the justice of her cause. And they say that ever after, while the Eagle's eggs lie in the nest in spring, the Beetle still sleeps in the ground. For so Jupiter commanded.

Even the weakest may find means to avenge a wrong.

THE EAGLE AND THE BEETLE

THE OLD LION AND THE FOX

An old Lion, whose teeth and claws were so worn that it was not so easy for him to get food as in his younger days, pretended that he was sick. He took care to let all his neighbors know about it, and then lay down in his cave to wait for visitors. And when they came to offer him their sympathy, he ate them up one by one.

The Fox came too, but he was very cautious about it. Standing at a safe distance from the cave, he inquired politely after the Lion's health. The Lion replied that he was very ill indeed, and asked the Fox to step in for a moment. But Master Fox very wisely stayed outside, thanking the Lion very kindly for the invitation.

"I should be glad to do as you ask," he added, "but I have noticed that there are many footprints leading into your cave and none coming out. Pray tell me, how do your visitors find their way out again?"

Take warning from the misfortunes of others.

THE MAN AND THE LION

A Lion and a Man chanced to travel in company through the forest. They soon began to quarrel, for each of them boasted that he and his kind were far superior to the other both in strength and mind.

Now they reached a clearing in the forest and there stood a statue. It was a representation of Heracles in the act of tearing the jaws of the Nemean Lion.

"See," said the man, "that's how strong *we* are! The King of Beasts is like wax in our hands!"

"Ho!" laughed the Lion, "a Man made that statue. It would have been quite a different scene had a Lion made it!"

It all depends on the point of view, and who tells the story.

THE ASS AND THE LAP DOG

There was once an Ass whose Master also owned a Lap Dog. This Dog was a favorite and received many a pat and kind word from his Master, as well as choice bits from his plate. Every day the Dog would run to meet the Master, frisking playfully about and leaping up to lick his hands and face.

All this the Ass saw with much discontent. Though he was well fed, he had much work to do; besides, the Master hardly ever took any notice of him.

Now the jealous Ass got it into his silly head that all he had to do to win his Master's favor was to act like the Dog. So one day he left his stable and clattered eagerly into the house.

Finding his Master seated at the dinner table, he kicked up his heels and, with a loud bray, pranced giddily around the table, upsetting it as he did so. Then he planted his forefeet on his Master's knees and rolled out his tongue to lick the Master's face, as he had seen the Dog do. But his weight upset the chair, and Ass and man rolled over together in the pile of broken dishes from the table.

The Master was much alarmed at the strange behavior of the Ass, and calling for help, soon attracted the attention of the servants. When they saw the danger the Master was in from the clumsy beast, they set upon the Ass and drove him with kicks and blows back to the stable. There they left him to mourn the foolishness that had brought him nothing but a sound beating.

Behavior that is regarded as agreeable in one is very rude and impertinent in another.

Do not try to gain favor by acting in a way that is contrary to your own nature and character.

THE MILKMAID AND HER PAIL

A Milkmaid had been out to milk the cows and was returning from the field with the shining milk pail balanced nicely on her head. As she walked along, her pretty head was busy with plans for the days to come.

"This good, rich milk," she mused, "will give me plenty of cream to churn. The butter I make I will take to market, and with the money I get for it I will buy a lot of eggs for hatching. How nice it will be when they are all hatched and the yard is full of fine young chicks. Then when May day comes I will sell them, and with the money I'll buy a lovely new dress to wear to the fair. All the young men will look at me. They will come and try to make love to me,—but I shall very quickly send them about their business!"

As she thought of how she would settle that matter, she tossed her head scornfully, and down fell the pail of milk to the ground. And all the milk flowed out, and with it vanished butter and eggs and chicks and new dress and all the milkmaid's pride.

Do not count your chickens before they are hatched.

THE WOLF AND THE SHEPHERD

A Wolf, lurking near the Shepherd's hut, saw the Shepherd and his family feasting on a roasted lamb.

"Aha!" he muttered. "What a great shouting and running about there would have been, had they caught me at just the very thing they are doing with so much enjoyment!"

Men often condemn others for what they see no wrong in doing themselves.

THE GOATHERD AND THE GOAT

A Goat strayed away from the flock, tempted by a patch of clover. The Goatherd tried to call it back, but in vain. It would not obey him. Then he picked up a stone and threw it, breaking the Goat's horn.

The Goatherd was frightened.

"Do not tell the master," he begged the Goat.

"No," said the Goat, "that broken horn can speak for itself!"

Wicked deeds will not stay hid.

THE MISER

A Miser had buried his gold in a secret place in his garden. Every day he went to the spot, dug up the treasure and counted it piece by piece to make sure it was all there. He made so many trips that a Thief, who had been observing him, guessed what it was the Miser had hidden, and one night quietly dug up the treasure and made off with it.

When the Miser discovered his loss, he was overcome with grief and despair. He groaned and cried and tore his hair.

A passerby heard his cries and asked what had happened.

"My gold! O my gold!" cried the Miser, wildly, "someone has robbed me!"

"Your gold! There in that hole? Why did you put it there? Why did you not keep it in the house where you could easily get it when you had to buy things?"

"Buy!" screamed the Miser angrily. "Why, I never touched the gold. I couldn't think of spending any of it."

The stranger picked up a large stone and threw it into the hole.

"If that is the case," he said, "cover up that stone. It is worth just as much to you as the treasure you lost!"

A possession is worth no more than the use we make of it.

THE WOLF AND THE HOUSE DOG

There was once a Wolf who got very little to eat because the Dogs of the village were so wide awake and watchful. He was really nothing but skin and bones, and it made him very downhearted to think of it.

One night this Wolf happened to fall in with a fine fat House Dog who had wandered a little too far from home. The Wolf would gladly have eaten him then and there, but the House Dog looked strong enough to leave his marks should he try it. So the Wolf spoke very humbly to the Dog, complimenting him on his fine appearance.

"You can be as well-fed as I am if you want to," replied the Dog. "Leave the woods; there you live miserably. Why, you have to fight hard for every bite you get. Follow my example and you will get along beautifully."

"What must I do?" asked the Wolf.

"Hardly anything," answered the House Dog. "Chase people who carry canes, bark at beggars, and fawn on the people of the house. In return you will get tidbits of every kind, chicken bones, choice bits of meat, sugar, cake, and much more beside, not to speak of kind words and caresses."

The Wolf had such a beautiful vision of his coming happiness that he almost wept. But just then he noticed that the hair on the Dog's neck was worn and the skin was chafed.

"What is that on your neck?"

"Nothing at all," replied the Dog.

"What! nothing!"

"Oh, just a trifle!"

"But please tell me."

"Perhaps you see the mark of the collar to which my chain is fastened."

"What! A chain!" cried the Wolf. "Don't you go wherever you please?"

"Not always! But what's the difference?" replied the Dog.

"All the difference in the world! I don't care a rap for your feasts and I wouldn't take all the tender young lambs in the world at that price." And away ran the Wolf to the woods.

There is nothing worth so much as liberty.

THE FOX AND THE HEDGEHOG

A Fox, swimming across a river, was barely able to reach the bank, where he lay bruised and exhausted from his struggle with the swift current. Soon a swarm of blood-sucking flies settled on him; but he lay quietly, still too weak to run away from them.

A Hedgehog happened by. "Let me drive the flies away," he said kindly.

"No, no!" exclaimed the Fox, "do not disturb them! They have taken all they can hold. If you drive them away, another greedy swarm will come and take the little blood I have left."

Better to bear a lesser evil than to risk a greater in removing it.

THE BAT AND THE WEASELS

A Bat blundered into the nest of a Weasel, who ran up to catch and eat him. The Bat begged for his life, but the Weasel would not listen.

"You are a Mouse," he said, "and I am a sworn enemy of Mice. Every Mouse I catch, I am going to eat!"

"But I am not a Mouse!" cried the Bat. "Look at my wings. Can Mice fly? Why, I am only a Bird! Please let me go!"

The Weasel had to admit that the Bat was not a Mouse, so he let him go. But a few days later, the foolish Bat went blindly into the nest of another Weasel. This Weasel happened to be a bitter enemy of Birds, and he soon had the Bat under his claws, ready to eat him.

"You are a Bird," he said, "and I am going to eat you!"

"What," cried the Bat, "I, a Bird! Why, all Birds have feathers! I am nothing but a Mouse. 'Down with all Cats,' is *my* motto!"

And so the Bat escaped with his life a second time.

Set your sails with the wind.

THE QUACK TOAD

An old Toad once informed all his neighbors that he was a learned doctor. In fact he could cure anything. The Fox heard the news and hurried to see the Toad. He looked the Toad over very carefully.

"Mr. Toad," he said, "I've been told that you cure anything! But just take a look at yourself, and then try some of your own medicine. If you can cure yourself of that blotchy skin and that rheumatic gait, someone might believe you. Otherwise, I should advise you to try some other profession."

Those who would mend others, should first mend themselves.

THE FOX WITHOUT A TAIL

A Fox that had been caught in a trap, succeeded at last, after much painful tugging, in getting away. But he had to leave his beautiful bushy tail behind him.

For a long time he kept away from the other Foxes, for he knew well enough that they would all make fun of him and crack jokes and laugh behind his back. But it was hard for him to live alone, and at last he thought of a plan that would perhaps help him out of his trouble.

He called a meeting of all the Foxes, saying that he had something of great importance to tell the tribe.

When they were all gathered together, the Fox Without a Tail got up and made a long speech about those Foxes who had come to harm because of their tails.

This one had been caught by hounds when his tail had become entangled in the hedge. That one had not been able to run fast enough because of the weight of his brush. Besides, it was well known, he said, that men hunt Foxes simply for their tails, which they cut off as prizes of the hunt. With such proof of the danger and uselessness of

having a tail, said Master Fox, he would advise every Fox to cut it off, if he valued life and safety.

When he had finished talking, an old Fox arose, and said, smiling:

"Master Fox, kindly turn around for a moment, and you shall have your answer."

When the poor Fox Without a Tail turned around, there arose such a storm of jeers and hooting, that he saw how useless it was to try any longer to persuade the Foxes to part with their tails.

Do not listen to the advice of him who seeks to lower you to his own level.

THE MISCHIEVOUS DOG

There was once a Dog who was so ill-natured and mischievous that his Master had to fasten a heavy wooden clog about his neck to keep him from annoying visitors and neighbors. But the Dog seemed to be very proud of the clog and dragged it about noisily as if he wished to attract everybody's attention. He was not able to impress anyone.

"You would be wiser," said an old acquaintance, "to keep quietly out of sight with that clog. Do you want everybody to know what a disgraceful and ill-natured Dog you are?"

Notoriety is not fame.

THE ROSE AND THE BUTTERFLY

A Butterfly once fell in love with a beautiful Rose. The Rose was not indifferent, for the Butterfly's wings were powdered in a charming pattern of gold and silver. And so, when he fluttered near and told how he loved her, she blushed rosily and said yes. After much pretty love-making and many whispered vows of constancy, the Butterfly took a tender leave of his sweetheart.

But alas! It was a long time before he came back to her.

"Is this your constancy?" she exclaimed tearfully. "It is ages since you went away, and all the time, you have been carrying on with all sorts of flowers. I saw you kiss Miss Geranium, and you fluttered around Miss Mignonette until Honey Bee chased you away. I wish he had stung you!"

"Constancy!" laughed the Butterfly. "I had no sooner left you than I saw Zephyr kissing you. You carried on scandalously with Mr. Bumble Bee and you made eyes at every single Bug you could see. You can't expect any constancy from me!"

Do not expect constancy in others if you have none yourself.

THE ROSE AND THE BUTTERFLY

THE CAT AND THE FOX

Once a Cat and a Fox were traveling together. As they went along, picking up provisions on the way—a stray mouse here, a fat chicken there—they began an argument to while away the time between bites. And, as usually happens when comrades argue, the talk began to get personal.

"You think you are extremely clever, don't you?" said the Fox. "Do you pretend to know more than I? Why, I know a whole sackful of tricks!"

"Well," retorted the Cat, "I admit I know one trick only, but that one, let me tell you, is worth a thousand of yours!"

Just then, close by, they heard a hunter's horn and the yelping of a pack of hounds. In an instant the Cat was up a tree, hiding among the leaves.

"This is my trick," he called to the Fox. "Now let me see what yours are worth."

But the Fox had so many plans for escape he could not decide which one to try first. He dodged here and there with the hounds at his heels. He doubled on his tracks, he ran at top speed, he entered a dozen burrows,—but all in vain. The hounds caught him, and soon put an end to the boaster and all his tricks.

Common sense is always worth more than cunning.

THE BOY AND THE NETTLE

A Boy, stung by a Nettle, ran home crying, to get his mother to blow on the hurt and kiss it.

"Son," said the Boy's mother, when she had comforted him, "the next time you come near a Nettle, grasp it firmly, and it will be as soft as silk."

Whatever you do, do with all your might.

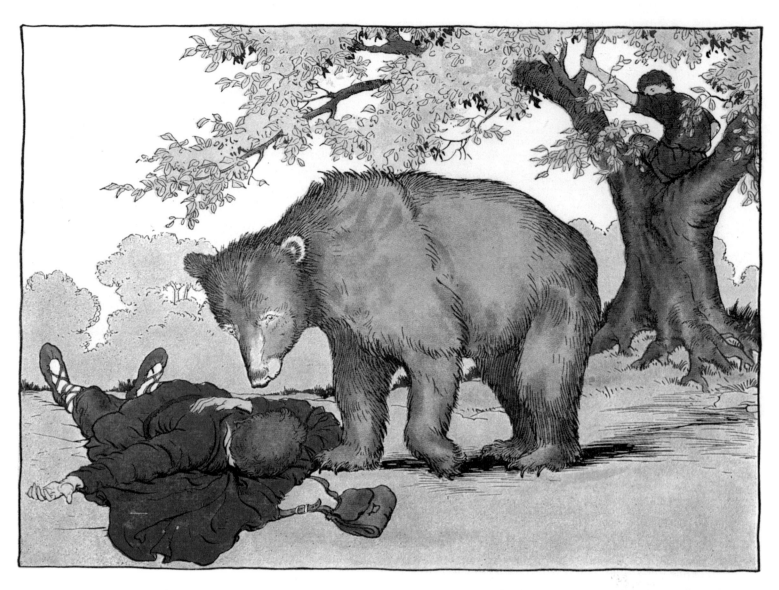

TWO TRAVELERS AND A BEAR

Two Men were traveling in company through a forest, when, all at once, a huge Bear crashed out of the brush near them.

One of the Men, thinking of his own safety, climbed a tree.

The other, unable to fight the savage beast alone, threw himself on the ground and lay still, as if he were dead. He had heard that a Bear will not touch a dead body.

It must have been true, for the Bear snuffed at the Man's head awhile, and then, seeming to be satisfied that he was dead, walked away.

The Man in the tree climbed down.

"It looked just as if that Bear whispered in your ear," he said. "What did he tell you?"

"He said," answered the other, "that it was not at all wise to keep company with a fellow who would desert his friend in a moment of danger."

Misfortune is the test of true friendship.

THE DOG AND HIS REFLECTION

A Dog, to whom the butcher had thrown a bone, was hurrying home with his prize as fast as he could go. As he crossed a narrow footbridge, he happened to look down and saw himself reflected in the quiet water as if in a mirror. But the greedy Dog thought he saw a real Dog carrying a bone much bigger than his own.

If he had stopped to think he would have known better. But instead of thinking, he dropped his bone and sprang at the Dog in the river, only to find himself swimming for dear life to reach the shore. At last he managed to scramble out, and as he stood sadly thinking about the good bone he had lost, he realized what a stupid Dog he had been.

It is very foolish to be greedy.

THE HARE AND THE TORTOISE

A Hare was making fun of the Tortoise one day for being so slow.

"Do you ever get anywhere?" he asked with a mocking laugh.

"Yes," replied the Tortoise, "and I get there sooner than you think. I'll run you a race and prove it."

The Hare was much amused at the idea of running a race with the Tortoise, but for the fun of the thing he agreed. So the Fox, who had consented to act as judge, marked the distance and started the runners off.

The Hare was soon far out of sight, and to make the Tortoise feel very deeply how ridiculous it was for him to try a race with a Hare, he lay down beside the course to take a nap until the Tortoise should catch up.

The Tortoise meanwhile kept goingly slowly but steadily, and, after a time, passed the place where the Hare was sleeping. But the Hare slept on very peacefully; and when at last he did wake up, the Tortoise was near the goal. The Hare now ran his swiftest, but he could not overtake the Tortoise in time.

The race is not always to the swift.

THE HARE AND THE TORTOISE

THE CAT AND THE OLD RAT

There was once a Cat who was so watchful, that a Mouse hardly dared show the tip of his whiskers for fear of being eaten alive. That Cat seemed to be everywhere at once with his claws all ready for a pounce. At last the Mice kept so closely to their dens, that the Cat saw he would have to use his wits well to catch one. So one day he climbed up on a shelf and hung from it, head downward, as if he were dead, holding himself up by clinging to some ropes with one paw.

When the Mice peeped out and saw him in that position, they thought he had been hung up there in punishment for some misdeed. Very timidly at first they stuck out their heads and sniffed about carefully. But as nothing stirred, all trooped joyfully out to celebrate the death of the Cat.

Just then the Cat let go his hold, and before the Mice recovered from their surprise, he had made an end of three or four.

Now the Mice kept more strictly at home than ever. But the Cat, who was still hungry for Mice, knew more tricks than one. Rolling himself in flour until he was covered completely, he lay down in the flour bin, with one eye open for the Mice.

Sure enough, the Mice soon began to come out. To the Cat it was almost as if he already had a plump young Mouse under his claws, when an old Rat, who had had much experience with Cats and traps, and had even lost a part of his tail to pay for it, sat up at a safe distance from a hole in the wall where he lived.

"Take care!" he cried. "That may be a heap of meal, but it looks to me very much like the Cat. Whatever it is, it is wisest to keep at a safe distance."

The wise do not let themselves be tricked a second time.

THE FOX AND THE CROW

One bright morning as the Fox was following his sharp nose through the wood in search of a bite to eat, he saw a Crow on the limb of a tree overhead. This was by no means the first Crow the Fox had ever seen. What caught his attention this time and made him stop for a second look, was that the lucky Crow held a bit of cheese in her beak.

"No need to search any farther," thought sly Master Fox. "Here is a dainty bite for my breakfast."

Up he trotted to the foot of the tree in which the Crow was sitting, and looking up admiringly, he cried, "Good-morning, beautiful creature!"

The Crow, her head cocked on one side, watched the Fox suspiciously. But she kept her beak tightly closed on the cheese and did not return his greeting.

"What a charming creature she is!" said the Fox. "How her feathers shine! What a beautiful form and what splendid wings! Such a wonderful Bird should have a very lovely voice, since everything else about her is so perfect. Could she sing just one song, I know I should hail her Queen of Birds."

Listening to these flattering words, the Crow forgot all her suspicion, and also her breakfast. She wanted very much to be called Queen of Birds.

So she opened her beak wide to utter her loudest caw, and down fell the cheese straight into the Fox's open mouth.

"Thank you," said Master Fox sweetly, as he walked off. "Though it is cracked, you have a voice sure enough. But where are your wits?"

The flatterer lives at the expense of those who will listen to him.

THE ANT AND THE DOVE

A Dove saw an Ant fall into a brook. The Ant struggled in vain to reach the bank, and in pity, the Dove dropped a blade of straw close beside it. Clinging to the straw like a shipwrecked sailor to a broken spar, the Ant floated safely to shore.

Soon after, the Ant saw a man getting ready to kill the Dove with a stone. But just as he cast the stone, the Ant stung him in the heel, so that the pain made him miss his aim, and the startled Dove flew to safety in a distant wood.

A kindness is never wasted.

THE MAN AND THE SATYR

A long time ago a Man met a Satyr in the forest and succeeded in making friends with him. The two soon became the best of comrades, living together in the Man's hut. But one cold winter evening, as they were walking homeward, the Satyr saw the Man blow on his fingers.

"Why do you do that?" asked the Satyr.

"To warm my hands," the Man replied.

When they reached home the Man prepared two bowls of porridge. These he placed steaming hot on the table, and the comrades sat down very cheerfully to enjoy the meal. But much to the Satyr's surprise, the Man began to blow into his bowl of porridge.

"Why do you do that?" he asked.

"To cool my porridge," replied the Man.

The Satyr sprang hurriedly to his feet and made for the door.

"Goodby," he said, "I've seen enough. A fellow that blows hot and cold in the same breath cannot be friends with me!"

The man who talks for both sides is not to be trusted by either.

THE MAN AND THE SATYR

THE LION'S SHARE

A long time ago, the Lion, the Fox, the Jackal, and the Wolf agreed to go hunting together, sharing with each other whatever they found.

One day the Wolf ran down a Stag and immediately called his comrades to divide the spoil.

Without being asked, the Lion placed himself at the head of the feast to do the carving, and, with a great show of fairness, began to count the guests.

"One," he said, counting on his claws, "that is myself, the Lion. Two, that's the Wolf, three, is the Jackal, and the Fox makes four."

He then very carefully divided the Stag into four equal parts.

"I am King Lion," he said, when he had finished, "so of course I get the first part. This next part falls to me because I am the strongest; and *this* is mine because I am the bravest."

He now began to glare at the others very savagely. "If any of you have any claim to the part that is left," he growled, stretching his claws meaningly, "now is the time to speak up."

Might makes right.

THE MOLE AND HIS MOTHER

A little Mole once said to his Mother:

"Why, Mother, you said I was blind! But I am sure I can see!"

Mother Mole saw she would have to get such conceit out of his head. So she put a bit of frankincense before him and asked him to tell what it was.

The little Mole peered at it.

"Why, that's a pebble!"

"Well, my son, that proves you've lost your sense of smell as well as being blind."

Boast of one thing and you will be found lacking in that and a few other things as well.

THE NORTH WIND
AND THE SUN

The North Wind and the Sun had a quarrel about which of them was the stronger. While they were disputing with much heat and bluster, a Traveler passed along the road wrapped in a cloak.

"Let us agree," said the Sun, "that he is the stronger who can strip that Traveler of his cloak."

"Very well," growled the North Wind, and at once sent a cold, howling blast against the Traveler.

With the first gust of wind the ends of the cloak whipped about the Traveler's body. But he immediately wrapped it closely around him, and the harder the Wind blew, the tighter he held it to him. The North Wind tore angrily at the cloak, but all his efforts were in vain.

Then the Sun began to shine. At first his beams were gentle, and in the pleasant warmth after the bitter cold of the North Wind, the Traveler unfastened his cloak and let it hang loosely from his shoulders. The Sun's rays grew warmer and warmer. The man took off his cap and mopped his brow. At last he became so heated that he pulled off his cloak, and, to escape the blazing sunshine, threw himself down in the welcome shade of a tree by the roadside.

Gentleness and kind persuasion win where force and bluster fail.

THE WOLF, THE KID, AND THE GOAT

Mother Goat was going to market one morning to get provisions for her household, which consisted of but one little Kid and herself.

"Take good care of the house, my son," she said to the Kid, as she carefully latched the door. "Do not let anyone in, unless he gives you this password: 'Down with the Wolf and all his race!'"

Strangely enough, a Wolf was lurking near and heard what the Goat had said. So, as soon as Mother Goat was out of sight, up he trotted to the door and knocked.

"Down with the Wolf and all his race," said the Wolf softly.

It was the right password, but when the Kid peeped through a crack in the door and saw the shadowy figure outside, he did not feel at all easy.

"Show me a white paw," he said, "or I won't let you in."

A white paw, of course, is a feature few Wolves can show, and so Master Wolf had to go away as hungry as he had come.

"You can never be too sure," said the Kid, when he saw the Wolf making off to the woods.

Two sureties are better than one.

THE SWALLOW AND THE CROW

The Swallow and the Crow had an argument one day about their plumage.

Said the Swallow: "Just look at my bright and downy feathers. Your black stiff quills are not worth having. Why don't you dress better? Show a little pride!"

"Your feathers may do very well in spring," replied the Crow, "but—I don't remember ever having seen you around in winter, and that's when I enjoy myself most."

Friends in fine weather only, are not worth much.

THE COCK AND THE FOX

A Fox was caught in a trap one fine morning, because he had got too near the Farmer's hen house. No doubt he was hungry, but that was not an excuse for stealing. A Cock, rising early, discovered what had happened. He knew the Fox could not get at him, so he went a little closer to get a good look at his enemy.

The Fox saw a slender chance of escape.

"Dear friend," he said, "I was just on my way to visit a sick relative, when I stumbled into this string and got all tangled up. But please do not tell anybody about it. I dislike causing sorrow to anybody, and I am sure I can soon gnaw this string to pieces."

But the Cock was not to be so easily fooled. He soon roused the whole hen yard, and when the Farmer came running out, that was the end of Mr. Fox.

The wicked deserve no aid.

THE ASS IN THE LION'S SKIN

An Ass found a Lion's skin left in the forest by a hunter. He dressed himself in it, and amused himself by hiding in a thicket and rushing out suddenly

at the animals who passed that way. All took to their heels the moment they saw him.

The Ass was so pleased to see the animals running away from him, just as if he were King Lion himself, that he could not keep from expressing his delight by a loud, harsh bray. A Fox, who ran with the rest, stopped short as soon as he heard the voice. Approaching the Ass, he said with a laugh:

"If you had kept your mouth shut you might have frightened me, too. But you gave yourself away with that silly bray."

A fool may deceive by his dress and appearance, but his words will soon show what he really is.

THE BEES AND WASPS, AND THE HORNET

A store of honey had been found in a hollow tree, and the Wasps declared positively that it belonged to them. The Bees were just as sure that the treasure was theirs. The argument grew very pointed, and it looked as if the affair could not be settled without a battle, when at last, with much good sense, they agreed to let a judge decide the matter. So they brought the case before the Hornet, justice of the peace in that part of the woods.

When the Judge called the case, witnesses declared that they had seen certain winged creatures in the neighborhood of the hollow tree, who hummed loudly, and whose bodies were striped, yellow and black, like Bees.

Counsel for the Wasps immediately insisted that this description fitted his clients exactly.

Such evidence did not help Judge Hornet to any decision, so he adjourned court for six weeks to give him time to think it over. When the case came up again, both sides had a large number of witnesses. An Ant was first to take the stand, and was about to be cross-examined, when a wise old Bee addressed the Court.

"Your honor," he said, "the case has now been pending for six weeks. If it is not decided soon, the honey will not be fit for anything. I move that the Bees and the Wasps be both instructed to build a honey comb. Then we shall soon see to whom the honey really belongs."

The Wasps protested loudly. Wise Judge Hornet quickly understood why they did so: They knew they could not build a honey comb and fill it with honey.

"It is clear," said the Judge, "who made the comb and who could not have made it. The honey belongs to the Bees."

Ability proves itself by deeds.

THE LARK AND HER YOUNG ONES

A Lark made her nest in a field of young wheat. As the days passed, the wheat stalks grew tall and the young birds, too, grew in strength. Then one day, when the ripe golden grain waved in the breeze, the Farmer and his son came into the field.

"This wheat is now ready for reaping," said the Farmer. "We must call in our neighbors and friends to help us harvest it."

The young Larks in their nest close by were much frightened, for they knew they would be in great danger if they did not leave the nest before the reapers came. When the Mother Lark returned with food for them, they told her what they had heard.

"Do not be frightened, children," said the Mother Lark. "If the Farmer said he would call in his neighbors and friends to help him do his work, this wheat will not be reaped for a while yet."

A few days later, the wheat was so ripe, that when the wind shook the stalks, a hail of wheat grains came rustling down on the young Larks' heads.

"If this wheat is not harvested at once," said the Farmer, "we shall lose half the crop. We

cannot wait any longer for help from our friends. Tomorrow we must set to work, ourselves."

When the young Larks told their mother what they had heard that day, she said:

"Then we must be off at once. When a man decides to do his own work and not depend on any one else, then you may be sure there will be no more delay."

There was much fluttering and trying out of wings that afternoon, and at sunrise next day, when the Farmer and his son cut down the grain, they found an empty nest.

Self-help is the best help.